This book was created for

You

May you be blessed with the gift
of knowing and appreciating who you are.

Dedication and Acknowledgements

You Are... is dedicated to God and our beloved children: Von Kai Rodriguera, Zan Aven Rodriguera and Bowie James Miguel. Thank you for inspiring us to create this book and for being the light in our hearts. Thank you to Gil Rodriguera and Joseph Sommer for loving and supporting us through this process. Thank you to our wonderful graphic designer, Yolanda Fundora, for using such care and expertise in helping to make our vision a reality. We are also very grateful to our families and friends for all the support, encouragement and feedback. It's because of you that we were able to complete this project. We love you!

Text ©2013 Chara Rodriguera
Illustrations ©2013 Jodi Bonthron

Book design by: Yolanda V. Fundora / www.urban-amish.com

All rights reserved. No part of this book may be reproduced or transmitted in any form whatsoever without the written permission of the publisher except in the case of brief quotations embodied in critical articles and reviews.

For more information regarding permission, write to: chara@solazzare.com

You Are...
12 empowering messages that celebrate you!

Written by: Chara Rodriguera

Illustrated by: Jodi Bonthron

Welcome Friend,

Thank you for taking the time to experience *You Are…*

This book is an invitation to celebrate YOU and your unique journey of living life to the fullest. We hope these words and images bring you great confidence and the inspiration to enjoy being exactly who you are.

You are amazing! So believe in yourself and always follow your heart!

With love and gratitude,

Chara and Jodi

Ideas for using this book:

You can use this book in any way that works for you. You can flip through it and see what catches your eye or you can read it from start to finish. Try any of the practices that sound fun or interesting. One idea is to pick a message that speaks to you and focus on it for a whole week or even a month. It takes about a month to create a new habit or thought pattern. Repetition is one of the best ways to instill empowering messages. The more you see and hear a message, the more it becomes part of your thought process. You will find a free download of all twelve messages on our website. You can print them out and put them where you will see them each day!

Benefits of Breathing Deeply:

It's suggested to breathe deeply throughout the book. Breathing deeply while you read and reflect on these empowering messages can help you:

- Be more present.
- Reduce anxiety and stress.
- Calm your mind.
- Enhance your focus and concentration.
- Create positive new thought patterns.
- And much more.

Parents and Guardians:

Sharing this book with your child is a great way to invest in your relationship and their well-being. It can begin a meaningful and ongoing dialogue that cultivates awareness, respect and connection. There is plenty of room for you to expand on these ideas and share your personal insights with your child. As you reflect and practice with your child, you may find that you experience your own positive shifts. It's a great way to discover and grow together!

For more information and inspiration please visit: Youareyouhaveyoucan.com

You are...

Amazing

#1
You are Amazing!

Amazing means magnificent, special, wondrous and surprising. Breathe deeply and know that you are amazing. You are bright like the sun, mysterious like the night, colorful like a rainbow and infinite like the sky. You have a body that can do amazing things. You have a mind that can think amazing thoughts. You have a spirit that is here to shine and live an amazing life. Inside you are seeds of greatness for you to discover and share with the world. You are on your very own amazing adventure called life. You will experience joys, disappointments, achievements and challenges. Yet, no matter what ups and downs occur, always remember that there is no limit to who you are, what you have and what you can do. By understanding that you are amazing, you can understand that all people are amazing in their own way.

REFLECTIONS:

1. What does the word amazing mean to you?
2. Think of someone you love. What is amazing about that person?
3. What is amazing about you?
4. How can you remind yourself each day that you are amazing?

PRACTICES:

1. Breathe deeply each morning, noon and night remembering that you are amazing.
2. Throughout your day, be on the lookout for things that are amazing.
3. Create a picture, poem, story or song about something you think is amazing.
4. Enjoy reading the affirmation to the right as often as possible for a week or even a month. Two great times are first thing in the morning and right before bed.

I am Amazing!

Amazing means magnificent, special, wondrous and surprising. I breathe deeply and know that I am amazing. I am bright like the sun, mysterious like the night, colorful like a rainbow and infinite like the sky. I have a body that can do amazing things. I have a mind that can think amazing thoughts. I have a spirit that is here to shine and live an amazing life. Inside me are seeds of greatness for me to discover and share with the world. I am on my very own amazing adventure called life. I willl experience joys, disappointments, achievements and challenges. Yet, no matter what ups and downs occur, I always remember that there is no limit to who I am, what I have and what I can do. By understanding that I am amazing, I can understand that all people are amazing in their own way.

#2 You are Unique!

Unique means one of a kind. You are a true original and no one else in the entire world is exactly like you. Breathe deeply and appreciate all the things about you that are unique. You have a personality, a style and a viewpoint that are all your own. You have special gifts and talents that only you can share. You have your own unique path and calling in your heart. Only you can create, express, dream, communicate, live and love like you can. You do not need to be like anyone else, nor does anyone else need to be like you. This is a blessing because it allows you the freedom to enjoy being your true self. By understanding that you are unique, you can respect and value the uniqueness in others.

REFLECTIONS:

1. What does the word unique mean to you?
2. What is unique and special about you?
3. How can you remind yourself each day that being unique is a blessing?

PRACTICES:

1. Breathe deeply each morning, noon and night remembering that you are unique.
2. Look for what is unique and special about each person you meet.
3. Enjoy reading the affirmation to the right as often as possible for a week or even a month. Two great times are first thing in the morning and right before bed.

I am Unique!

Unique means one of a kind. I am a true original and no one else in the entire world is exactly like me. I breathe deeply and appreciate all the things about me that are unique. I have a personality, a style and a viewpoint that are all my own. I have special gifts and talents that only I can share. I have my own unique path and calling in my heart. Only I can create, express, dream, communicate, live and love like I can. I do not need to be like anyone else, nor does anyone else need to be like me. This is a blessing because it allows me the freedom to enjoy being my true self. By understanding that I am unique, I can respect and value the uniqueness in others.

Beautiful

#3
You are Beautiful!

Beautiful means lovely and exquisite. Breathe deeply and connect to the beauty that is within you and around you. There are so many different types of beauty. A rose is beautiful and a wildflower is beautiful in a different way. A swan is beautiful and a stallion is beautiful in a different way. The ocean is beautiful and mountains are beautiful in a different way. Everything and everyone in the world has their own kind of beauty. It's not your size, color, shape, age or style that's important. Your true beauty is unique to you and cannot be compared to any one else. You are beautiful simply because you are you. The more you love yourself and take good care of yourself, the more your true beauty shines through. By recognizing that you are beautiful, you can recognize that all people are beautiful in their own special way.

REFLECTIONS:

1. What does the word beautiful mean to you?
2. Think of someone you love. What is beautiful about that person?
3. What is beautiful about you?
4. How can you remind yourself each day that you are beautiful?

PRACTICES:

1. Breathe deeply each morning, noon and night remembering that you are beautiful.
2. Notice all the things in life that are beautiful.
3. Create a collage of things that are beautiful to you.
4. Enjoy reading the affirmation to the right as often as possible for a week or even a month. Two great times are first thing in the morning and right before bed.

I am Beautiful!

Beautiful means lovely and exquisite. I breathe deeply and connect to the beauty that is within me and around me. There are so many different types of beauty. It's not my size, color, shape, age or style that's important. My true beauty is unique to me and cannot be compared to any one else. I am beautiful simply because I am me. The more I love myself and take good care of myself, the more my true beauty shines through. By recognizing that I am beautiful, I can recognize that all people are beautiful in their own special way.

You are...

Intelligent

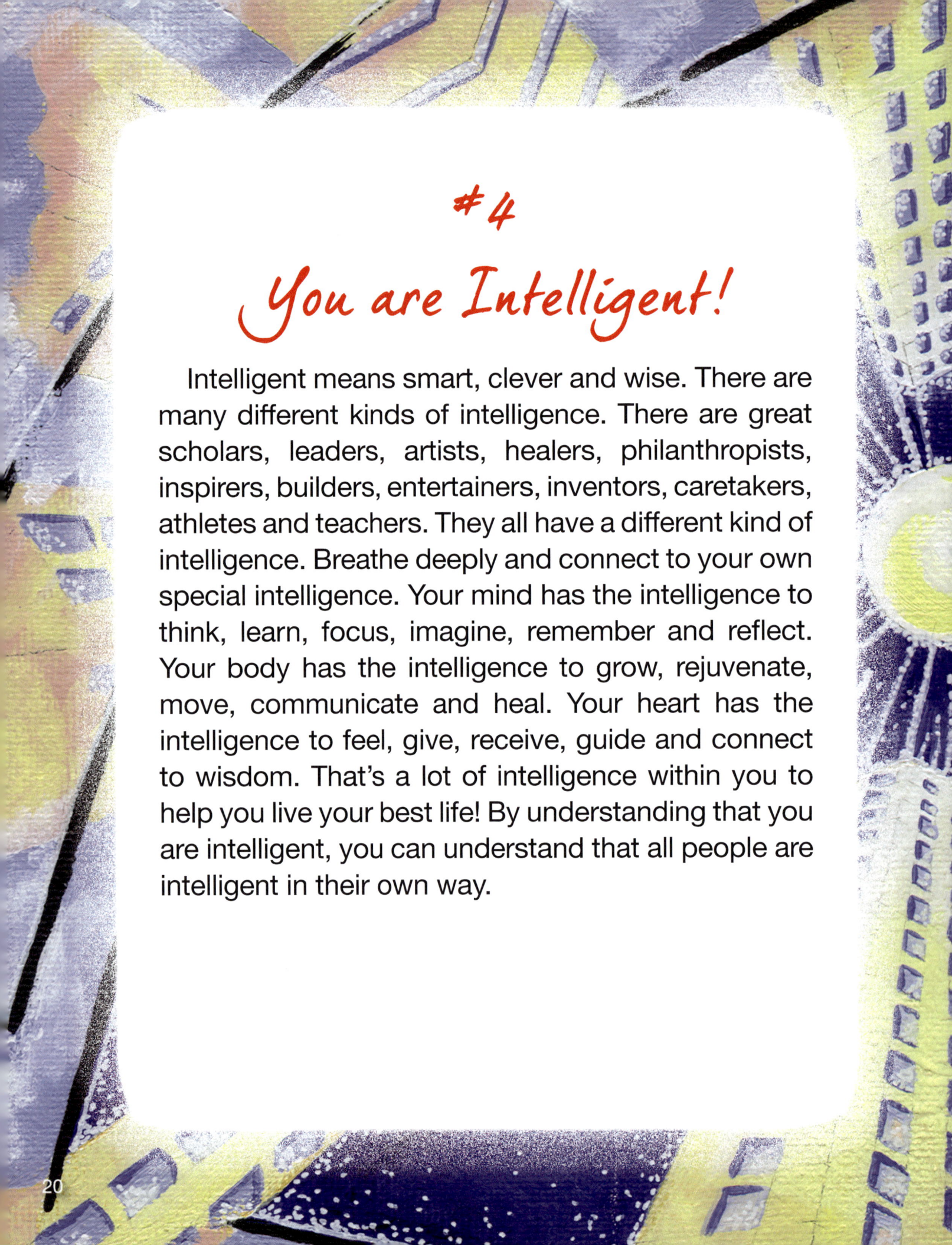

#4 You are Intelligent!

Intelligent means smart, clever and wise. There are many different kinds of intelligence. There are great scholars, leaders, artists, healers, philanthropists, inspirers, builders, entertainers, inventors, caretakers, athletes and teachers. They all have a different kind of intelligence. Breathe deeply and connect to your own special intelligence. Your mind has the intelligence to think, learn, focus, imagine, remember and reflect. Your body has the intelligence to grow, rejuvenate, move, communicate and heal. Your heart has the intelligence to feel, give, receive, guide and connect to wisdom. That's a lot of intelligence within you to help you live your best life! By understanding that you are intelligent, you can understand that all people are intelligent in their own way.

REFLECTIONS:

1. What does the word intelligent mean to you?
2. In what ways are you intelligent?
3. How can you use your intelligence each day?

PRACTICES:

1. Breathe deeply each morning, noon and night remembering that you are intelligent.
2. Notice and appreciate when you or someone else does or says something intelligent.
3. Enjoy reading the affirmation to the right as often as possible for a week or even a month. Two great times are first thing in the morning and right before bed.

I am Intelligent!

Intelligent means smart, clever and wise. There are many different kinds of intelligence. I breathe deeply and connect to my own special intelligence. My mind has the intelligence to think, learn, focus, imagine, remember and reflect. My body has the intelligence to grow, rejuvenate, move, communicate and heal. My heart has the intelligence to feel, give, receive, guide and connect to wisdom. That's a lot of intelligence within me to help me live my best life! By understanding that I am intelligent, I can understand that all people are intelligent in their own way.

You are...

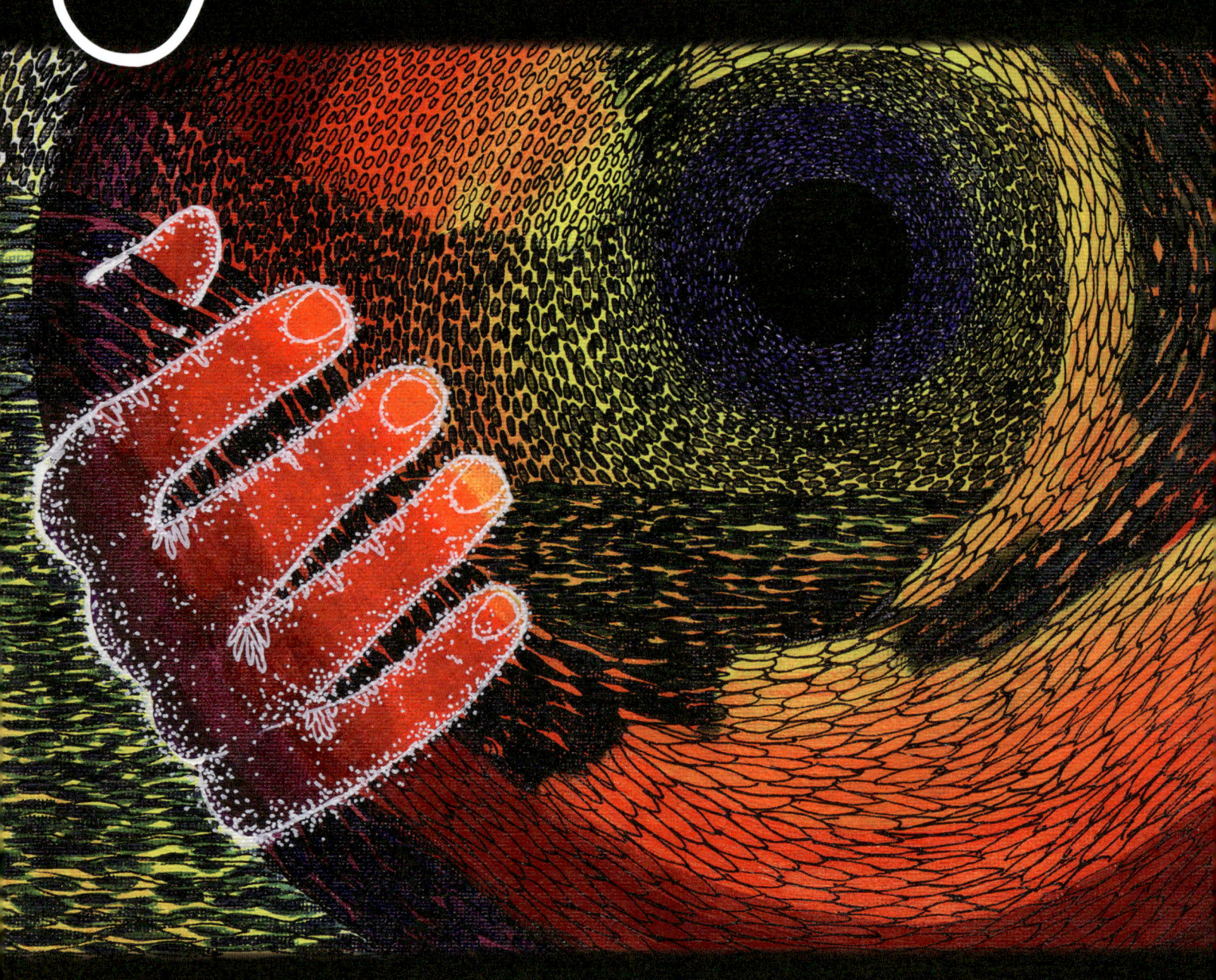

Creative

#5
You are Creative!

Creative means fresh, new and innovative. Breathe deeply and connect to your creative energy. Inside you is an artist, a writer, a dancer, a singer, a musician, a builder, a designer and an inventor. You are a creator and your creativity is a way to share yourself with the world. Not only in an artistic sense, but also in the way that you approach life, handle challenges and communicate with others. To be creative is to think outside the box by making something new or doing something in a new way. To be creative is to know that you can make something special out of any thing or any situation. Being creative is like having magical powers because you have the ability to make whatever you choose. One of the greatest things you can create is an extraordinary life. By understanding that you are creative, you can understand that all people are creative in their own way.

REFLECTIONS:

1. What does the word creative mean to you?
2. In what ways do you enjoy being creative?
3. How can you use your creativity each day?

PRACTICES:

1. Breathe deeply each morning, noon and night remembering that you are creative.
2. Take a class or practice one of your favorite creative activities.
3. Do one thing in a new way each day.
4. Enjoy reading the affirmation to the right as often as possible for a week or even a month. Two great times are first thing in the morning and right before bed.

I am Creative!

Creative means fresh, new and innovative. I breathe deeply and connect to my creative energy. Inside me is an artist, a writer, a dancer, a singer, a musician, a builder, a designer and an inventor. I am a creator and my creativity is a way to share myself with the world. Not only in an artistic sense, but also in the way that I approach life, handle challenges and communicate with others. To be creative is to think outside the box by making something new or doing something in a new way. To be creative is to know that I can make something special out of any thing or any situation. Being creative is like having magical powers because I have the ability to make whatever I choose. One of the greatest things I can create is an extraordinary life. By understanding that I am creative, I can understand that all people are creative in their own way.

You are...

#6
You are Talented!

Talented means having a special skill or ability. Your talents are gifts for you to enjoy and share with the world. Breathe deeply and remember that you are talented. You are good at so many things and there are a few things that you are extra good at doing. It's important to recognize that even things you do naturally and easily are still talents that deserve to be valued. Throughout your life, you will discover and develop more talents, as well as learn how to put them to good use. You can share your special abilities with people in order to help them or bring them joy. When you share your talents, it's like giving a gift to others and to yourself at the same time. By recognizing and sharing your talents, you can recognize and appreciate other people's talents too.

REFLECTIONS:

1. What does the word talented mean to you?
2. What are some of your special talents?
3. How can you use and share your talents each day?

PRACTICES:

1. Breathe deeply each morning, noon and night remembering that you are talented.
2. Practice or take lessons to improve your talents.
3. Encourage others to share their talents.
4. Enjoy reading the affirmation to the right as often as possible for a week or even a month. Two great times are first thing in the morning and right before bed.

I am Talented!

Talented means having a special skill or ability. My talents are gifts for me to enjoy and share with the world. I breathe deeply and remember that I am talented. I am good at so many things and there are a few things that I am extra good at doing. It's important to recognize that even things I do naturally and easily are still talents that deserve to be valued. Throughout my life, I will discover and develop more talents, as well as learn how to put them to good use. I can share my special abilities with people in order to help them or bring them joy. When I share my talents, it's like giving a gift to others and to myself at the same time. By recognizing and sharing my talents, I can recognize and appreciate other people's talents too.

You are...

Growing

#7
You are Growing!

Growing means to expand or get bigger. Each day you are learning, discovering and evolving for the better. Breathe deeply and know that you are growing. You are a work in progress – a masterpiece in the making! You are perfect just as you are. Yet, you can practice things you want to do better. You can also be curious about things you want to learn. With each new day of exploration, you are growing into your best self. You are like a plant that starts out as a little seed and grows into a stem, roots, leaves and blossoms. There's no need to rush your growing process because each part of your journey is important and valuable. If you stumble or make a mistake, be gentle with yourself and practice doing better next time. By understanding that you are growing, you can understand that every person is learning and growing too.

REFLECTIONS:

1. What does the word growing mean to you?
2. In what ways are you growing and learning?
3. How can you remind yourself each day that you are growing?

PRACTICES:

1. Breathe deeply each morning, noon and night remembering that you are growing.
2. Be understanding if you or someone else makes a mistake. Remember that everyone is learning and growing.
3. Enjoy reading the affirmation to the right as often as possible for a week or even a month. Two great times are first thing in the morning and right before bed.

I am Growing!

Growing means to expand or get bigger. Each day I am learning, discovering and evolving for the better. I breathe deeply and know that I am growing. I am a work in progress – a masterpiece in the making! I am perfect just as I am. Yet, I can practice things I want to do better. I can also be curious about things I want to learn. With each new day of exploration, I am growing into my best self. I am like a plant that starts out as a little seed and grows into a stem, roots, leaves and blossoms. There's no need to rush my growing process because each part of my journey is important and valuable. If I stumble or make a mistake, I can be gentle with myself and practice doing better next time. By understanding that I am growing, I can understand that every person is learning and growing too.

#8
You are Powerful!

Powerful means strong and capable. Breathe deeply and know that you are powerful. You have the power of your body, your mind and your spirit. You have the power to choose your thoughts, words and actions. You have the power to decide if it's best to speak or listen, lead or follow, take action or wait. You have the power to encourage rather than criticize, to help rather than harm, to focus on solutions rather than problems. If you fall down, you have the power to get back up. If you get stuck, you have the power to ask for help. Most of all, you have the power to know what's right for you and live a life that represents what's important to your heart. As you discover how powerful you are, you discover that all people are powerful too.

REFLECTIONS:

1. What does the word powerful mean to you?
2. Think of someone you love. In what way is that person powerful?
3. In what ways are you powerful?
4. How can you remind yourself each day that you are powerful?

PRACTICES:

1. Breathe deeply each morning, noon and night remembering that you are powerful.
2. Use your power to encourage or help someone. Notice how this makes you feel.
3. Enjoy reading the affirmation to the right as often as possible for a week or even a month. Two great times are first thing in the morning and right before bed.

I am Powerful!

Powerful means strong and capable. I breathe deeply and know that I am powerful. I have the power of my body, my mind and my spirit. I have the power to choose my thoughts, words and actions. I have the power to decide if it's best to speak or listen, lead or follow, take action or wait. I have the power to encourage rather than criticize, to help rather than harm, to focus on solutions rather than problems. If I fall down, I have the power to get back up. If I get stuck, I have the power to ask for help. Most of all, I have the power to know what's right for me and live a life that represents what's important to my heart. As I discover how powerful I am, I discover that all people are powerful too.

You are...

#9
You are Infinite!

Infinite means endless and unlimited. It means there is no limit to your potential and what is possible for you. Breathe deeply and know that you are infinite. There is no limit to who you are or who you can become. There is no limit to what you can learn and discover. There is no limit to what you can imagine and accomplish. Even if something doesn't work out the way you want, there is always another way you can look at it, another idea you can try and another direction you can go. There may be something about you or your life that you wish were different. However, what you have or don't have does not define you or what is possible for you. Any challenge you face can teach you something and inspire you to be more and do more than you thought you could. By understanding that you are infinite, you can understand that all people are infinite too.

REFLECTIONS:

1. What does the word infinite mean to you?
2. Is there anything about you or your life that you wish were different? If so, come up with some new ideas about how you can look at it.
3. How can you remind yourself each day that you are infinite?

PRACTICES:

1. Breathe deeply each morning, noon and night remembering that you are infinite.
2. Spend a few minutes each day looking at the infinite sky and notice how you feel.
3. Enjoy reading the affirmation to the right as often as possible for a week or even a month. Two great times are first thing in the morning and right before bed.

I am Infinite!

Infinite means endless and unlimited. It means there is no limit to my potential and what is possible for me. I breathe deeply and know that I am infinite. There is no limit to who I am or who I can become. There is no limit to what I can learn and discover. There is no limit to what I can imagine and accomplish. Even if something doesn't work out the way I want, there is always another way I can look at it, another idea I can try and another direction I can go. There may be something about me or my life that I wish were different. However, what I have or don't have does not define me or what is possible for me. Any challenge I face can teach me something and inspire me to be more and do more than I thought I could. By understanding that I am infinite, I can understand that all people are infinite too.

You are...

Connected

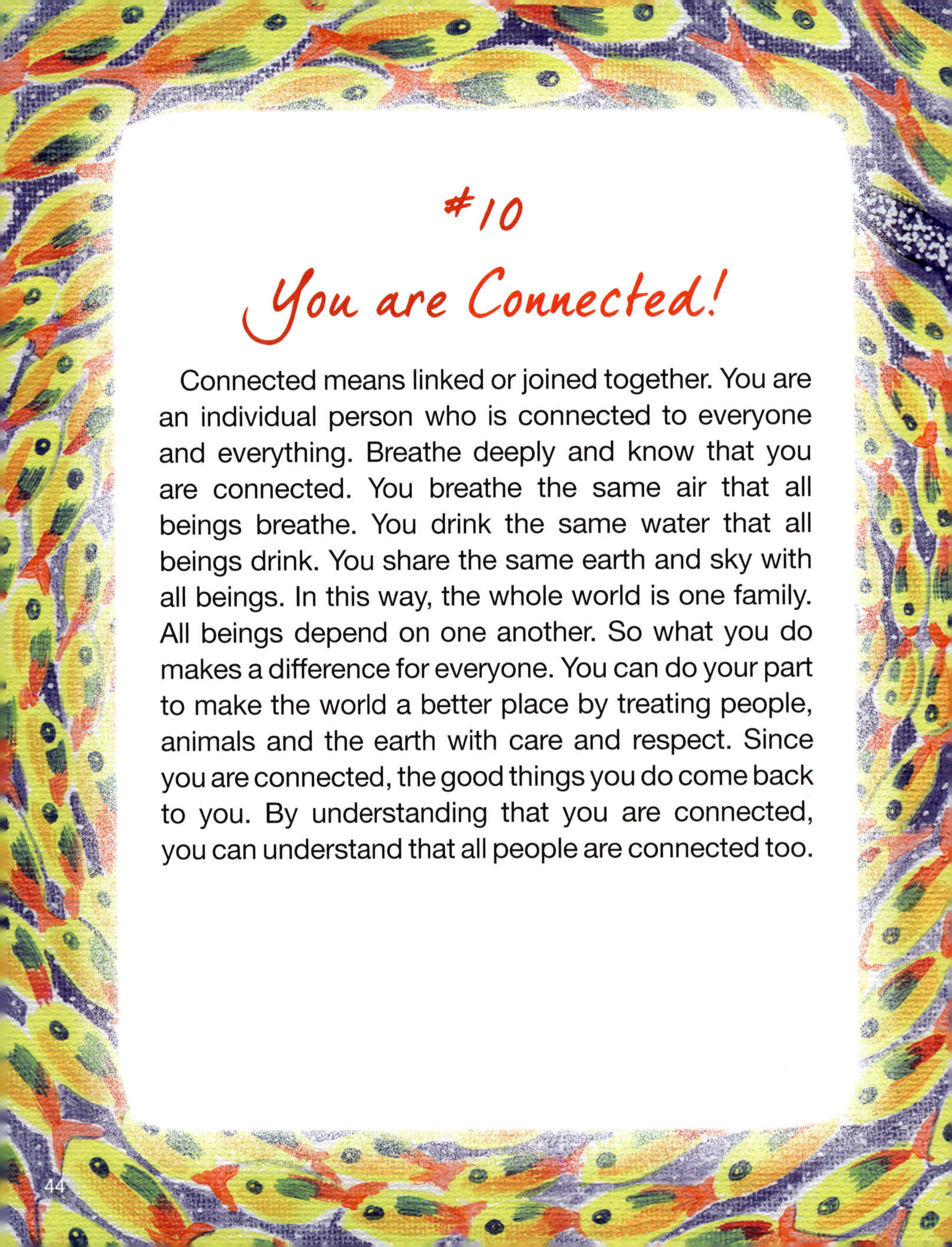

#10
You are Connected!

Connected means linked or joined together. You are an individual person who is connected to everyone and everything. Breathe deeply and know that you are connected. You breathe the same air that all beings breathe. You drink the same water that all beings drink. You share the same earth and sky with all beings. In this way, the whole world is one family. All beings depend on one another. So what you do makes a difference for everyone. You can do your part to make the world a better place by treating people, animals and the earth with care and respect. Since you are connected, the good things you do come back to you. By understanding that you are connected, you can understand that all people are connected too.

REFLECTIONS:

1. What does the word connected mean to you?
2. How does it feel to be connected to someone you love?
3. What are some ways you can offer care and respect for people, animals and the earth?
4. How can you remind yourself each day that you are connected?

PRACTICES:

1. Breathe deeply each morning, noon and night remembering that you are connected.
2. Do at least one thing each day to show care for someone else.
3. Enjoy reading the affirmation to the right as often as possible for a week or even a month. Two great times are first thing in the morning and right before bed.

I am Connected!

Connected means linked or joined together. I am an individual person who is connected to everyone and everything. I breathe deeply and know that I am connected. I breathe the same air that all beings breathe. I drink the same water that all beings drink. I share the same earth and sky with all beings. In this way, the whole world is one family. All beings depend on one another. So what I do makes a difference for everyone. I can do my part to make the world a better place by treating people, animals and the earth with care and respect. Since I am connected, the good things I do come back to me. By understanding that I am connected, I can understand that all people are connected too.

You are...

a Miracle

#11
You are a Miracle!

A miracle is something remarkable, magical and divine. Breathe deeply and know that you are a true miracle. It's a miracle that after a storm you may find a beautiful rainbow illuminating the sky. It's a miracle that a tiny acorn grows into a mighty oak tree. It's a miracle that a crawling caterpillar transforms into a butterfly with wings. It's a miracle that there is only one you in the entire world for all time. You are more brilliant than any sunrise, more valuable than any treasure and more extraordinary than any work of art. You are a one of a kind masterpiece. You are a wish come true. Therefore, you are a gift to the world and a blessing to be cherished. Your life is something to appreciate and celebrate every single day! Even when things feel really, really hard, always remember that you are a miracle and your life is precious. By understanding that you are a miracle, you can understand that every person is a miracle too.

REFLECTIONS:

1. What does the word miracle mean to you?
2. Have you seen or heard about any miracles?
3. In what ways are you a miracle?
4. How can you remind yourself each day that you are miracle?

PRACTICES:

1. Breathe deeply each morning, noon and night remembering that you are a miracle.
2. Be on the look out for life's miracles.
3. Create a poem, story, picture or song about a special miracle.
4. Enjoy reading the affirmation to the right as often as possible for a week or even a month. Two great times are first thing in the morning and right before bed.

I am a Miracle!

A miracle is something remarkable, magical and divine. I breathe deeply and know that I am a true miracle. It's a miracle that there is only one me in the entire world for all time. I am more brilliant than any sunrise, more valuable than any treasure and more extraordinary than any work of art. I am a one of a kind masterpiece. I am a wish come true. Therefore, I am a gift to the world and a blessing to be cherished. My life is something to appreciate and celebrate every single day! Even when things feel really, really hard, I always remember that I am a miracle and my life is precious. By understanding that I am a miracle, I can understand that every person is a miracle too.

You are...

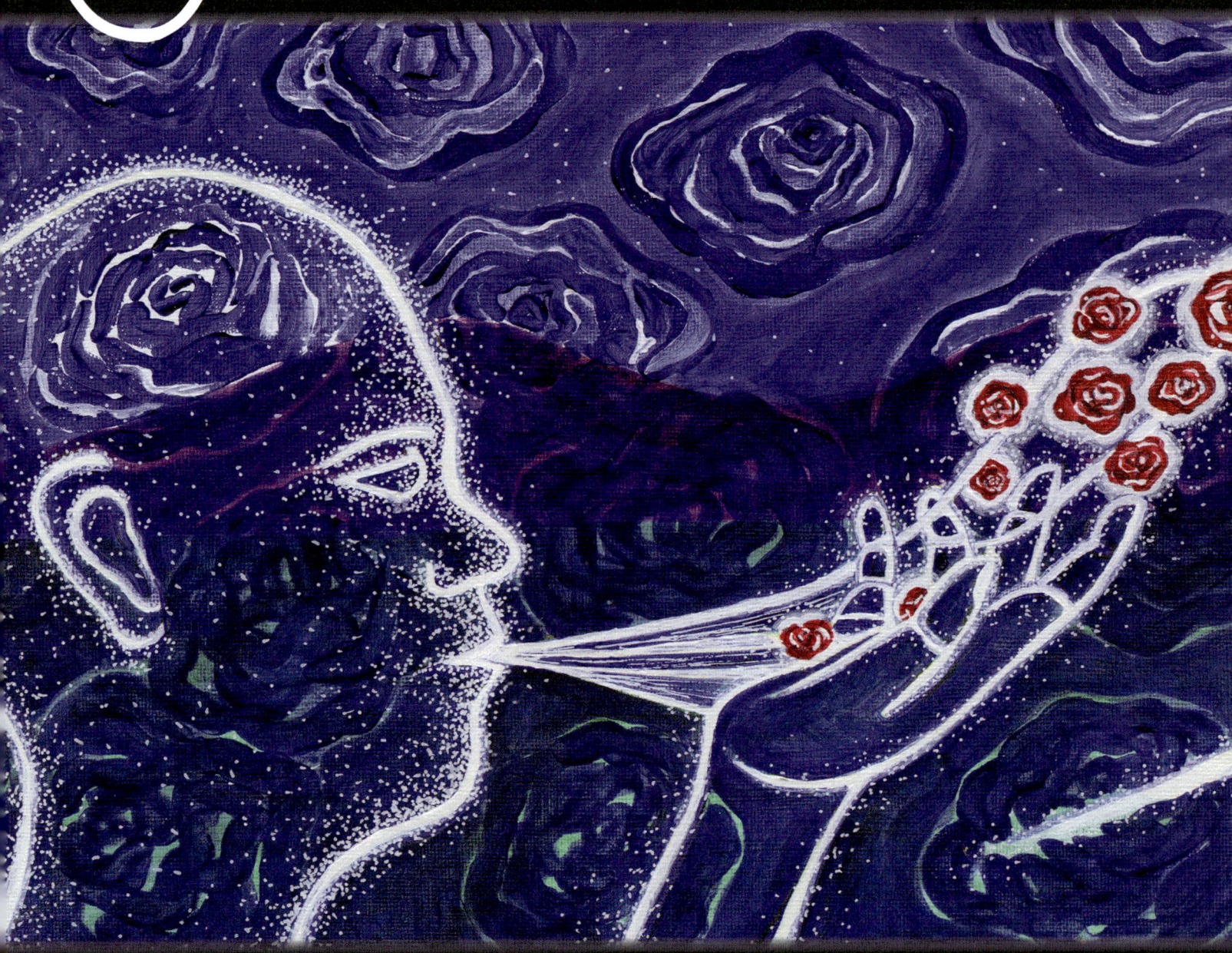

Love

#12
You are Love!

Love is the deepest form of affection, kindness, compassion and devotion. You were created from love. Therefore, love lives in your heart and is the very center of who you are. Breathe deeply and know that you are love. As a human being, you experience all kinds of emotions. Yet, behind the feelings that come and go, you will always find love shining. Just like you will always find the sun shining behind the clouds that come and go. Love is within you and around you at all times. If you feel upset or alone, you can look up at the vast sky and feel a loving presence. You can walk on the green grass and feel a loving presence. You can spend time with someone you care about and feel a loving presence. You can look into your own eyes and feel a loving presence. Breathe into your heart and allow the love inside you to expand. You have unlimited love to give and receive. By understanding that you are love, you can understand that each person is love too.

REFLECTIONS:

1. What does the word love mean to you?
2. In what ways do you receive love from others?
3. In what ways do you give love to yourself and others?
4. How can you remind yourself each day that you are love?

PRACTICES:

1. Breathe deeply each morning, noon and night remembering that you are love.
2. Create a list of everyone and everything you love and add to it each day.
3. Enjoy reading the affirmation to the right as often as possible for a week or even a month. Two great times are first thing in the morning and right before bed.

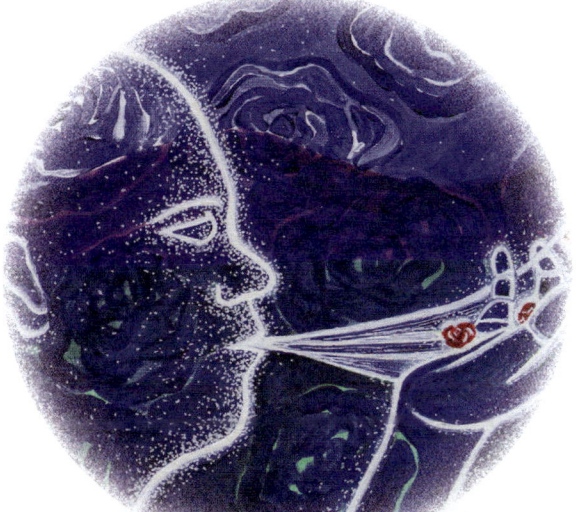

I am Love!

Love is the deepest form of affection, compassion, kindness and devotion. I was created from love. Therefore, love lives in my heart and is the very center of who I am. I breathe deeply and know that I am love. As a human being, I experience all kinds of emotions. Yet, behind the feelings that come and go, I will always find love shining. Just like I will always find the sun shining behind the clouds that come and go. Love is within me and around me at all times. If I feel upset or alone, I can look up at the vast sky and feel a loving presence. I can walk on the green grass and feel a loving presence. I can spend time with someone I care about and feel a loving presence. I can look into my own eyes and feel a loving presence. I breathe into my heart and allow the love inside me to expand. I have unlimited love to give and receive. By understanding that I am love, I can understand that each person is love too.

You are

all these wonderful messages
and much, much more!

The next pages are for you
to write, draw, collage, explore and play
with who YOU believe you are...
and who you wish to become.

Thank you for being you!

I am...

I am...

Chara

I am a Mother and an Inspirer. Some of my favorite ways to share inspiration are through writing, instructing yoga and life programs, creating guided meditations and producing media with a message. I originally began writing *You Are...* for my two sons, Von and Zan. Soon into the process, I felt a knowing in my heart that said, "These messages are not only for your sons. They are for every child - every human being." And so I felt guided, step by step, to create this book with my talented friend, Jodi. It comes from our hearts and the belief that we all are special, capable and divine.

Jodi

I am a mixed media artist and love my work as an art teacher. The photographs are of my son, Bowie, and myself in our work space. He is a miracle. His presence inspires me and reminds me that all things are possible with God.

I hope the paintings delight you, provoke your imagination and carry you to a new place within yourself.

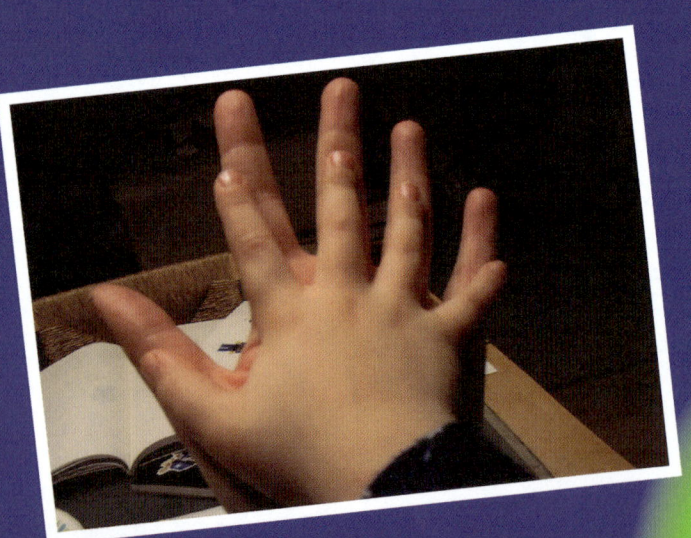

We look forward to sharing our next books with you:

You Have... & You Can...

For more information and inspiration please visit:
Youareyouhaveyoucan.com

Made in the USA
Charleston, SC
03 March 2017